The Atlantic Ocean

By **Leighton Taylor**

BLACKBIRCH PRESS, INC.

WOODBRIDGE, CONNECTICUT

TABLE OF CONTENTS

Published by Blackbirch Press, Inc.
260 Amity Road
Woodbridge, CT 06525

©1999 by Blackbirch Press, Inc.
First Edition

e-mail: staff@blackbirch.com
Web site: www.blackbirch.com

Photo credits are on p. 48.

Text ©Leighton Taylor
Printed in the United States

10 9 8 7 6 5 4 3 2

Editor's Note

The photos that appear on pages 38 and 41
show species that are found in the Atlantic
Ocean, but the photos were taken in a
different locale. Because no suitable images
of the species could be found in an Atlantic
environment, these very similar images were
used instead.

Library of Congress Cataloging-in-Publication Data

Taylor, L.R. (Leighton R.)
The Atlantic Ocean / by Leighton Taylor
     p.   cm. — (Life in the sea)
    Includes bibliographical references and index.
    Summary: Discusses the location, physical environment, life forms, and exploration of the Atlantic Ocean.
    ISBN 1-56711-246-3 (library binding : alk. paper)
    1. Oceanography—Atlantic Ocean—Juvenile literature. [1. Atlantic Ocean.] I. Title. II. Series: Taylor, L.R.
(Leighton R.) Life in the sea
GC481.T39 1999
578.773—dc21
                                                    98-49123
                                                  CIP
                                                     AC

IMAGINE AN OCEAN OF CORAL REEFS AND ICEBERGS

Imagine an ocean stretching in the shape of a fat 'S' from nearly the top of the planet to nearly the bottom. Deep beneath this ocean is a narrow curving spine of submarine mountains.

In the northern and southern ends of this body of water, there are floating icebergs big enough to sink a ship as gigantic as the *Titanic*. In the middle area, near the Equator, the ocean shallows host coral reefs with colorful fish and sharks.

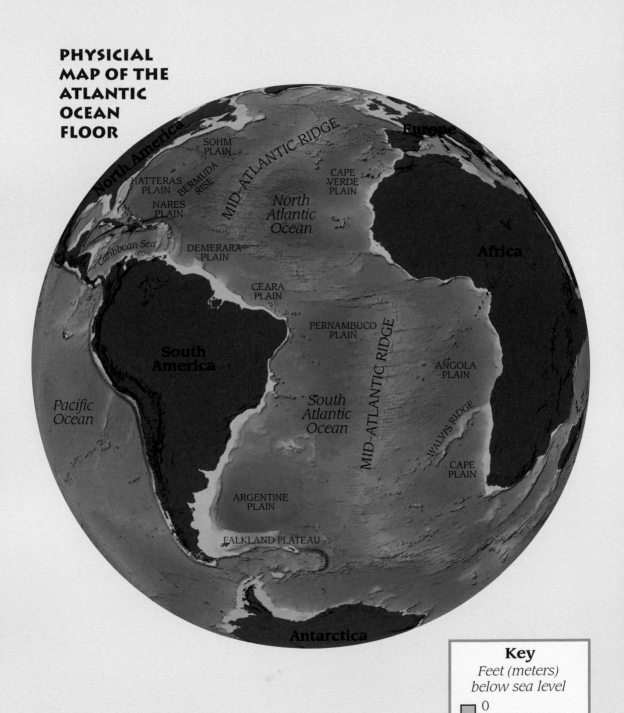

PHYSICIAL MAP OF THE ATLANTIC OCEAN FLOOR

North America

Europe

SOHM PLAIN

MID-ATLANTIC RIDGE

HATTERAS PLAIN

BERMUDA RISE

CAPE VERDE PLAIN

NARES PLAIN

North Atlantic Ocean

Africa

Caribbean Sea

DEMERARA PLAIN

CEARA PLAIN

PERNAMBUCO PLAIN

South America

ANGOLA PLAIN

MID-ATLANTIC RIDGE

Pacific Ocean

South Atlantic Ocean

WALVIS RIDGE

CAPE PLAIN

ARGENTINE PLAIN

FALKLAND PLATEAU

Antarctica

Key

Feet (meters) below sea level

0

5,000 (1,524)

10,000 (3,048)

IMAGINE AN OCEAN OF CORAL REEFS AND ICEBERGS

Imagine an ocean stretching in the shape of a fat 'S' from nearly the top of the planet to nearly the bottom. Deep beneath this ocean is a narrow curving spine of submarine mountains.

In the northern and southern ends of this body of water, there are floating icebergs big enough to sink a ship as gigantic as the *Titanic*. In the middle area, near the Equator, the ocean shallows host coral reefs with colorful fish and sharks.

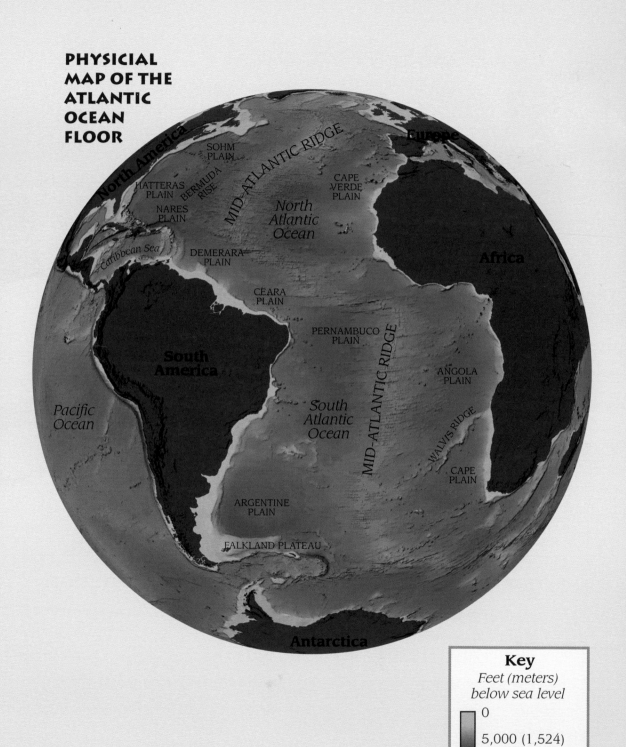

PHYSICAL
MAP OF THE
ATLANTIC
OCEAN
FLOOR

North America

SOHM
PLAIN

MID-ATLANTIC RIDGE

Europe

HATTERAS
PLAIN

BERMUDA
RISE

CAPE
VERDE
PLAIN

NARES
PLAIN

North
Atlantic
Ocean

Africa

Caribbean Sea

DEMERARA
PLAIN

CEARA
PLAIN

PERNAMBUCO
PLAIN

South
America

ANGOLA
PLAIN

Pacific
Ocean

South
Atlantic
Ocean

MID-ATLANTIC RIDGE

WALVIS RIDGE

CAPE
PLAIN

ARGENTINE
PLAIN

FALKLAND PLATEAU

Antarctica

Key

*Feet (meters)
below sea level*

0

5,000 (1,524)

10,000 (3,048)

EXPLORING THE OCEAN'S DEPTHS

But you don't have to imagine! There is such an ocean—the Atlantic Ocean—between North America and Europe, and between South America and Africa.

In Jules Verne's famous novel of undersea exploration—*20,000 Leagues Beneath the Sea*—the book's fictional hero, Captain Nemo, traveled around the world in his submarine named the *Nautilus*.

Let's imagine we have a ship like Captain Nemo's that travels around the Atlantic and beneath its surface. We can take a quick 20,000 mile (32,000 kilometer) trip around this ocean. We'll start near Iceland and head southeast to Scotland. We must beware of icebergs!

Here the ocean bottom is a rough mountain range, so we will stay in the green upper layers of the water. As we move south to Ireland, we notice the water has warmed up. Our sub has to work a little harder to sail against the Gulf Stream current that has come up from Florida and crossed the Atlantic.

Near the surface we see gray seals and harbor seals catching fish. As we head south toward Spain, on our left is the entrance to the English Channel. It takes ocean water into the North Sea.

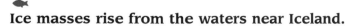

Ice masses rise from the waters near Iceland.

◀ **Rugged cliffs line the shores of Ireland's southwest coast.**

North of Spain, we sail through the Bay of Biscay. Here, 500 years ago, Basque fishermen hunted right whales and humpback whales. We keep going south along the coast of Spain. Finally, on our left is the Strait of Gibraltar where the Atlantic enters the Mediterranean Sea.

Heading southwest, we pass the Madeira Islands and the Canary Islands off the shores of Africa. Around these islands live rare Mediterranean monk seals. They only live here and in the Mediterranean, on the rocky shores of Turkey and Greece. We continue along the coast of Saharan Africa, past the Cape Verde Islands. Then we will go offshore and dive our sub more than a mile deep.

Down here, we can follow the Mid-Atlantic Ridge, the undersea range of mountains that form the spine of the Atlantic. We take a quick left to the tip of South Africa where we see a group of great white sharks chasing fur seals. And up on shore, three kinds of penguins are resting on the rocks.

Now, we turn right (heading west) and cross the widest part of the Atlantic—from the tip of South Africa to the tip of South America. About midway, we pass South Georgia Island. It is a large mid-ocean island with a mountain 9,000 feet (2,700 meters) above sea level. South Georgia Island is alive with marine life—sea birds, penguins, fur seals, and whales.

◄ **Elephant seals sunbathe on the warm rocks of the South American coast.**

We continue our sub-Atlantic journey west to the very tip of South America, called Cape Horn. Some of the roughest seas in the world are here. As we head north along the coast of Argentina, we can glimpse large bays where right whales swim with their calves. Fur seals and elephant seals sunbathe on the rocks. As we sail north, just off Buenos Aires and Montevideo, the water is very green and murky. The great river Plata enters the Atlantic here, draining part of the Amazon rain forest.

On the map:
North America
Iceland
Europe
MID-ATLANTIC RIDGE
North Atlantic Ocean
Africa
South America
South Atlantic Ocean
MID-ATLANTIC RIDGE

We keep going north along the coast of South America, past Rio de Janeiro to the point of Brazil. This land points eastward to a notch on the coast of Africa. Millions of years ago this piece of land fit up against Africa and there was no Atlantic Ocean. At this place, there is little continental shelf and the water drops to almost a mile deep, very close to shore. We continue up the coast of South America and the water again is murky and green. Here, the Amazon River drains more fresh water into the ocean than at any other place in the world.

High above Rio de Janeiro, Brazil's major business center.

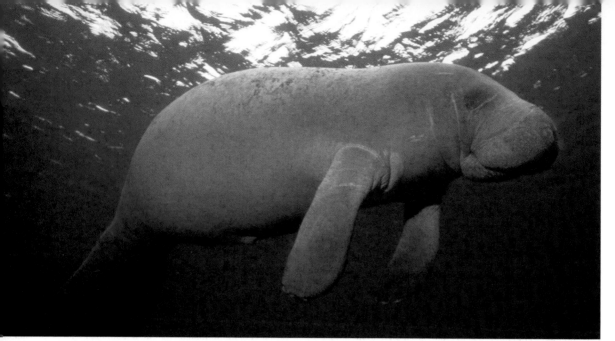

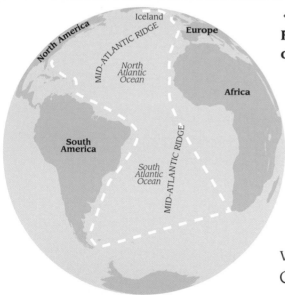

🐟 **Manatees can be found off the Florida coast, where the warm waters of the Gulf Stream meet the Atlantic.**

Near Puerto Rico, we can dive our submarine to the deepest part of the Atlantic Ocean. The Puerto Rico Trench is 28,232 feet (8,600 meters) deep. To our left is the warm Caribbean Sea. We won't visit there now, but will pass Cuba as we continue on toward Florida. We can feel our sub speed up because of the force of the warm Gulf Stream heading up the coast of the United States, north past Boston Harbor.

🐟 **The *Mayflower* sits in Plymouth Harbor in the Massachusetts Bay.**

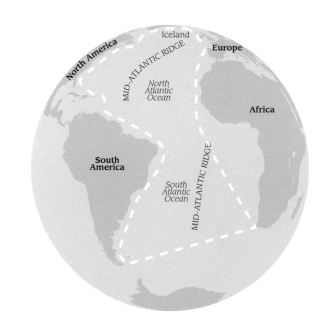

As we head northeast to Newfoundland, we can see round-headed white beluga whales. If we can get close to shore, we may be lucky enough to see gangs of walruses and perhaps even a polar bear. As we venture even farther into the North Atlantic, our submarine slows down as it's moved to the east by the cold Labrador Current. When this cold current meets the warm current of the Gulf Stream, the moist air forms fog.

We travel around the tip of Greenland and finally complete our journey in Iceland, back in iceberg territory again!

Above right: **Acadian Nova Scotia's shores are rugged and rocky.**
Below right: **Huge icebergs fill the waters near Greenland.**

THE NATURE OF THE OCEAN

When astronauts look at Earth from space, they see a planet mostly covered by water. Some people call our Earth "Planet Ocean." That's because it has much more ocean than dry land.

From space, the world's ocean looks the same all over. But it can be very different from place to place. The water can be different. The location and shape of the holes filled by seawater can be special.

How is seawater different from one place to another? Here are three important ways that seawater can change, depending on:

1. how warm or cold it is
2. how much salt it holds
3. how clear or murky it is

The surface seawater in the Atlantic Ocean has a great effect on the weather in the eastern United States, Canada, and Europe. The warm waters of the Gulf Stream flow up the coast of the United States and across the Atlantic to England and Ireland. Because of the warm Gulf Stream, the weather in these places is milder than areas without a warm current.

Oceanographers are scientists who study the ocean. Oceanographers can tell a lot about the currents in the Atlantic Ocean by using satellites. Cameras and instruments on satellites record the temperature, movement, and level of the ocean currents on the surface of the sea. Oceanographers also use ships to take water temperatures and measure ocean saltiness below the surface.

All this information helps them do many things—study currents and the winds, predict weather, help fishermen find fish, help sea captains save fuel, and a lot more.

This view from space— taken by *Apollo* astronauts—shows the Atlantic Ocean in between South America (lower left) and the western tip of Africa (upper right).

MORE THAN SEVEN SEAS—THE MANY WATERS OF THE WORLD

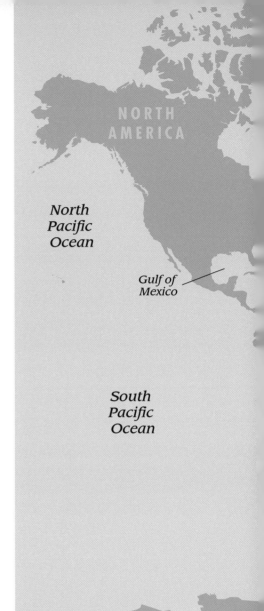

The location and shape of a basin filled by seawater gives each body of water special characteristics. The earth's seawater fits into holes of many different sizes and shapes. These giant holes are shaped by the land around them. The names for these different areas of seawater depend on their size and shape.

An *ocean* is the biggest area of seawater. An *ocean* is so big, it touches several continents. It can take many days to cross an ocean, even in a fast boat. The Pacific Ocean is the world's largest ocean. The Atlantic Ocean and the Indian Ocean are very large, too.

A *sea* is smaller than an ocean but still very big. A sea is more enclosed by land than an ocean and may touch only a few countries or even be in the middle of a single country. Sailing the "Seven Seas" is an old sailor's term. In reality, there are many more seas than seven. The Mediterranean Sea is a big, famous sea. It is connected to the Red Sea by the Suez Canal. The Caribbean Sea touches Florida and Mexico and has many islands.

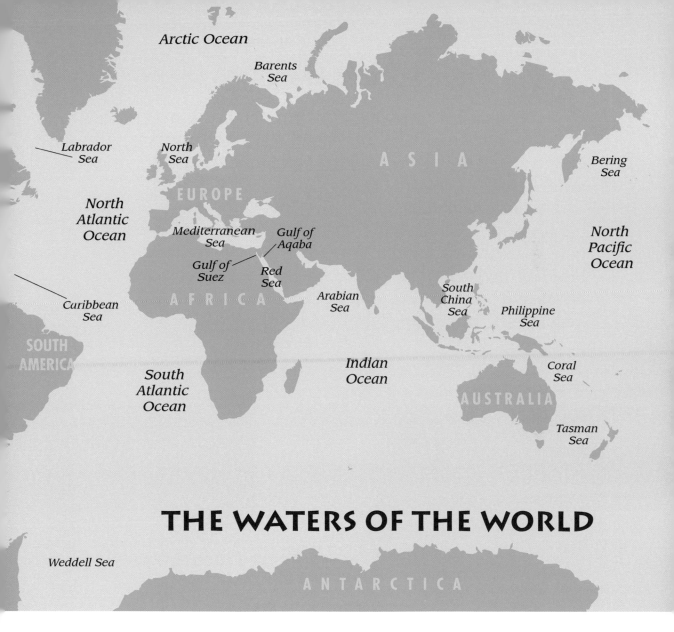

THE WATERS OF THE WORLD

Smaller parts of the ocean can be called a *gulf*. Sometimes gulfs are big, sometimes small. The Gulf of Mexico is very big. The Gulf of Aqaba (AH-ka-ba) and the Gulf of Suez are small. These gulfs are at the very top of the Red Sea.

TRUE BLUE CRABS

Most crabs crawl slowly on the ocean bottom or skitter quickly on rocks and beaches. They walk or run on the tips of eight long thin legs. But some crabs swim, too.

A famous swimming crab in the Atlantic Ocean is the blue crab. The scientific name (Callinectes) of the blue crab means "beautiful swimmer." How does this blue crab swim? Its rear pair of legs end in flattened paddles. A blue crab can leap up from the bottom and paddle itself through the water quite fast.

Blue crab

◄ **The rear walking legs of the blue crab have developed into swimming paddles.**

Blue crabs live all along the mid-southern coast of the United States. They are often most abundant in Chesapeake Bay, a large inlet of the Atlantic. The bay lies between the states of Maryland and Virginia. Blue crabs are good hunters. They use their strong claws to catch tiny fish, other crabs, shrimp, and even insects.

Blue crabs eat many kinds of creatures. But humans love to eat blue crabs. Over the years, more blue crabs have been fished from Chesapeake Bay than any other crab in the oceans. Now, we must be careful not to take too many.

SPINES AND CLAWS

Does a lobster have claws? Some do, and some don't. The kind of lobster that lives in colder Atlantic waters from Massachusetts to Maine has large, strong claws. Many people called these greenish bottom-dwellers "Maine lobsters." They are very good to eat. When Maine lobsters are cooked, they change color from green to red.

Across the Atlantic, off the coast of Ireland, lives another kind of lobster. It has no large front claws. It has long slender legs and spiny feelers. One name for these crustaceans is "spiny lobsters."

Spiny lobsters, common in the northeastern Atlantic, do not have large front claws.

THE BERMUDA TRIANGLE—
A WHALE OF A TALE

≈≈≈≈≈≈≈≈≈≈≈≈≈≈≈≈≈≈≈≈≈≈

Unproved myths and stories describe a mysterious, dangerous place in the Atlantic Ocean. Legends say the area is inside a triangle formed by three lines drawn between Florida, Puerto Rico, and Bermuda. Stories say that sometimes ships and planes lose their way in this big part of the ocean and can be lost forever. The truth is that there is no proof for these stories.

In fact, for hundreds of years, ocean explorers have used Bermuda as a helpful landmark for finding their way between Europe and North America.

Migrating whales (and maybe bluefin tuna, sharks, and other fish) also use Bermuda as a waypoint—a mid-ocean milestone. The islands of Bermuda are just the top of an undersea mountain that is more than 2 1/2 miles (4 kilometers) high. Whales can sense this undersea landmark by using a special sounding system called echolocation. To do this, blue whales make strong sounds. When the sounds hit the mountain, they bounce back to the whale. The farther away the whale is from the mountain, the longer the bounced sound takes to return. Such echoes help the whales navigate and find their way.

Using one common name ("lobster") for several different kinds of animals can be misleading. That's why biologists—and sometimes even fishermen—use scientific names. Most clawed lobsters belong to a group named Homarus. Most spiny lobsters belong to a group called Panulirus.

◀ Walruses like these used to inhabit the waters off Maine, Massachusetts, and Nova Scotia. Overhunting has reduced their population greatly.

WALRUSES IN MAINE? SEALS IN AFRICA?

Do you think walruses and seals only live in the icy waters of the Arctic? Well, that's not really true. Today, most walruses live in waters near the icy edge of the very northern part of the Atlantic Ocean and in the adjoining Arctic Ocean. Walruses use their long tusks to pull themselves up onto the ice. When they feed, they brace themselves on their tusks against the sandy or muddy ocean bottom. Using tusks as rails, walruses slide along the bottom sucking up clams and shrimp with their big lips.

Before humans overhunted walruses in the Atlantic, the rocky shores of Nova Scotia, Maine, and Massachusetts were home to these two-ton, leathery skinned clam eaters. Now the number of Atlantic walruses is dangerously low. To help ensure their survival, they are now protected by law.

How about seals? Of the kinds of seals that live in the North Atlantic, four (hooded, bearded, harp, and ringed) stay near the icy waters north off Nova Scotia. Two kinds (gray and harbor) live in the cold waters of Ireland, New England, and coastal France. But one kind, the Mediterranean monk seal, lives in the warm waters of the Atlantic, off the coast of North Africa and in the Canary Islands and Madeira. As its name suggests, this seal also lives in the warm Mediterranean Sea.

Unfortunately, the Mediterranean monk seal is almost extinct.

Some people and governments are trying to save them. But a few fishermen kill monk seals because they think they steal their fish. Sadly, Caribbean monk seals, relatives of Mediterranean monk seals, have not been seen since the 1950s. This species is probably extinct.

Harp seals are one of many seal species found in the northern Atlantic.

↢ **These humpback whales are lunge feeding, using their huge expandable mouths to suck up hundreds of gallons of small fish and shrimp.**

IS EVERY WHALE THE RIGHT WHALE?

The Atlantic Ocean is home to many kinds of whales, including sperm whales, humpback whales, minke whales, sei whales, and right whales. Sadly, the whale population has been severely lessened over the centuries by whaling and fishing practices. One species, the Atlantic gray whale, is probably extinct—never to be seen again.

When tourists go whale watching on a boat from Boston Harbor, or watch from a headland in Argentina, any whale they see might be the "right" whale for them because they have been looking so hard. But there really is a kind of whale called the right whale. The North Atlantic and the South Atlantic both have large groups, called populations, of right whales. Members of each population seldom, if ever, cross the Equator to join the neighboring population.

Right whales in both the North and South Atlantic migrate each year. During the winter, they go toward the Equator to warm water where they give birth to their calves and mate for the next season. When the weather warms up the water closer to the Poles, they go poleward to feeding areas thousands of miles away from their winter calving grounds.

Right whales in the North Atlantic spend the summer in waters near Maine and Massachusetts. As winter comes, they migrate south to the warmer waters of the Caribbean.

Right whales in the South Atlantic spend the winter months in bays along the coast of Argentina and Uruguay. As summer comes to the southern hemisphere (in November), they swim poleward toward the Antarctic where the waters are rich with food.

Below left: **Northern right whales spend their summers near Maine and their winters near the Caribbean.**
Below right: **Sperm whales are among the biggest whales in the Atlantic.**

GREAT COD ALMIGHTY

For centuries, one of the most valuable and common big fish in the North Atlantic Ocean was the Atlantic cod.

Cod can grow to six feet (1.8 meters) long and weigh 200 pounds (91 kilograms). They once lived in huge schools near the bottom on offshore banks—sandy and muddy undersea hills—near Massachusetts, Maine, Nova Scotia, and Newfoundland. Cod are brownish, spotted, and have white bellies. A small barbel (whisker) hangs down from a cod's chin.

Fishermen can dry cod into hard chunks that look like jerky because the meat is very low in fat. Dried cod can last for many months. Viking ships carried dried cod as "fuel" for the sailors to eat during their trips to England and the coast of North America. Later, in the 16th and 17th centuries, explorers from England, Holland, Spain, and Portugal fed their crews with dried cod.

Each mother cod produces millions and millions of eggs, but only a few survive. Most are eaten by other fish and ocean creatures. Still, there were once so many cod in the Atlantic that sailors bragged they could walk ashore on the backs of the fish!

For hundreds of years, fishermen caught cod with long, hooked lines and pulled them up by hand. Sometimes they used traps. It took a lot of work to catch cod. But in the 1950s, trouble started.

Many countries from all over the world sent giant factory ships to the North Atlantic Banks. They used huge nets to catch more and more cod.

Today, cod still live on the Banks. But so few are left that governments have closed fishing. The world can learn from the story of the Atlantic cod. We must be careful not to upset the delicate balance of the ocean and the life within it.

Left: **The waters off Cape Cod in Massachusetts have always been rich with fish of many species.**
Inset: **Atlantic Cod**

GALLOPING SCALLOPS

Have you ever seen a clam swim? Most clams, as well as their relatives—mussels, cockles, oysters—live in mud, sand, or are attached to rocks or pilings. They don't move around very fast at all.

Cockles—often found in mud or sand—are a common catch off the coast of Ireland.
Inset: A woman sells cockles in an Irish market.

But one of their relatives swims quite fast. This speedy cousin of the clam is called a scallop. Scallops live on rocky bottoms along the Atlantic coasts of the United States and Europe. The shells of scallops have a very familiar shape. A very well-known gasoline company uses it on all their signs. The two shells hold the scal-lop's body. A strong round muscle can pull the shell together and hold it tightly closed. (This round, white muscle is what fish markets and cafes sell as "scallops.")

Some scallops—like this Atlantic flame scallop—are brightly colored.

A scallop lays on its side—on one of the two shells—upon the ocean bottom. Around the open edge of its shell are a series of "eyes," most often they are blue. When a scal-lop's eyes see a threat—a hungry fish or skate—its muscles can push water out of the shell very fast. This jet of water propels the shell in a quick burst through the water so it can escape.

A SEA OF SEAWEED

Some Atlantic waters flow into pockets, called seas, that are almost entirely surrounded by land. Examples are the Irish Sea, the North Sea, the Mediterranean Sea, and the Caribbean Sea. But the Atlantic holds one sea that is far from land. The Sargasso Sea is a huge area of the Atlantic Ocean north of Cuba and east of North Carolina. A pattern of currents, including part of the Gulf Stream, forms what scientists call an 'eddy'. An eddy is a giant circle of slowly moving water. This eddy holds the water mass of the Sargasso Sea within it. The surface of the Sargasso Sea is almost completely covered by floating brown seaweed called Sargasso weed. Some kinds of sea animals are adapted for living in the Sargasso weed. Some examples are seahorses and the Sargasso anglerfish. Many kinds of open-ocean fish like tunas and mahi-mahi like to gather beneath the shade of the floating seaweed.

Sailors of the 16th and 17th century feared sailing into the Sargasso Sea because they thought the seaweed would stop their ships and hold them captive.

Opposite: **A young loggerhead turtle hatchling makes its way through the dense seaweed of the Sargasso Sea.**

THE MYSTERY OF THE DISAPPEARING EELS

Many rivers in Europe drain into the Atlantic Ocean. For centuries, people have caught big silvery eels in the fresh waters of the rivers. Eels have been a treasured food on Atlantic coasts probably since humans first found the shores. But in all that time no one ever saw a baby eel. Where did these eels come from? So interested were people in answering this question that a Danish beer company offered a big cash prize to the fisherman or scientist who solved this mystery.

It took many scientists a long time to finally find an answer. Here's what we know today: At about 5-12 years of age, big eels—longer than a man's arm—swim down their river into the open ocean. Then they head southwest, swimming toward the Sargasso Sea.

Deep down below the seaweed that floats on the surface, the eels mate and then die. The eggs they produce float around for a few days and then hatch into young eels. But they look very different from their parents. Baby eels, shorter than your little finger, are long, flat, and clear. If you caught one in a net, you could see its backbone. Young eels feed on tiny floating animals. They grow longer as they swim thousands of miles to return to the rivers where their parents lived.

Atlantic Anguilla eels. The reproduction process of many eels has been a longtime mystery.

After months and months of swimming, the eels reach their river. Quickly, in a few days, they change into a color and shape just like their parents. They swim up the river and (unless caught by a fisherman) live there for twelve years or so. Then they begin their return journey to the distant deep waters where they first started swimming.

A skate's mermaid's purse protects the developing animal.
Inset: An embryo grows inside the sturdy casing.

SECRETS IN A MERMAID'S PURSE

Walk along the beaches of the Atlantic Ocean, in the United States or Europe, and you may find a mermaid's purse. At least that's what people call the small, four-sided packets that wash up on the sand and dry in the sun. These rubbery, brownish purses are now empty, but they once held something special.

Mermaid's purses are really the flexible egg cases laid by some skates and certain sharks—cat sharks and chain dogfish.

Winter skate

Each egg case—usually smaller than a baseball card—once protected a single young skate or shark. When first laid by the mother, the egg case was nestled among seaweeds or wedged in a rocky crack on the ocean bottom. Like all egg cases, it held a yolk that was food for the tiny animal growing within it. As the skate or shark got larger, the food supply inside the egg case got smaller.

After several months, the young animal inside the flexible egg case was as least as big as your finger. With all its food used up, the animal had to wriggle out of the case and find food outside, by hunting.

Chain dogfish

GREAT WHITE, WHATTA SIGHT

The biggest, most dangerous shark in all the oceans of the world, including the Atlantic, is the great white shark. Great whites are already about 3 feet (1 meter) long when they are born. Their mothers may be longer than a taxi. The teeth of a great white shark are shaped like broad-based triangles. They have razor-sharp edges shaped like the blades of a steak knife, and are often found in rows of two or three. These dangerous teeth are handy for feeding on seals, whales, big fish—and very rarely—people.

People who had never heard of great white sharks discovered them in the movie and book, *Jaws*. The great white in that story lived in the waters of New England. But great white sharks live all around the world—in the Atlantic Ocean on all coasts, mainly in cooler waters from New England to Ireland to South America and West Africa. Great white sharks also have been seen off the coasts of Hawaii, Mexico, California, Oregon, and Washington.

Below: **Great Whites are the most dangerous—and most feared—sharks in the world.**
Opposite and inset: **The giant Atlantic manta ray is the largest living species of ray.**

SEE A RAY, IT'S OKAY

Unlike their highly feared cousin—the great white shark—rays are generally peaceful, quiet creatures. The giant manta ray—also called a "devilfish"—is the largest species of living ray. Some mantas have been known to grow to more than 2 tons and to have a wingspan exceeding 20 feet (6 meters). Despite its size, nickname, and reputation, the Atlantic manta is a gentle fish that spends much of its time cruising the upper waters of the Atlantic, searching for shellfish, small fishes, and plankton to eat.

S BANKS WITH OVERDRAWN ACCOUNTS

Several million years ago, the Atlantic Ocean did not exist. It was gradually formed by a huge land mass that split apart. Parts of this ocean still hold the richest fishing grounds in the world. People once saw schools of fish so big, their boats had to slow down to avoid running into them.

Some of the richest fishing areas in the world lie off the coasts of Maine, Nova Scotia, and Newfoundland. Called the Grand Banks, this shallow area on the edge of the continental shelf extends for miles and miles.

Beneath the surface of the Grand Banks, the water is filled with life that feeds on the rich food of tiny plants, fertilized by chemicals in the cold water. Part of the area extends southward to Georges Bank offshore from Cape Cod, Massachusetts.

Some of the world's richest fishing areas lie in the northern Atlantic, off the coast of Maine.

◀ **Herring (above) and mackerel (inset) are only two of the many species of food fish found in the Atlantic's northern waters.**

The Banks have long been home to such important food fish as cod, haddock, plaice, halibut, herring, and mackerel. Some warm water fish also follow the Gulf Stream into this rich area—swordfish, mako sharks, and large tuna are caught near the edges of the banks.

For many centuries, from the Vikings to the Pilgrims to Gloucester fishermen, people have pulled tons and tons of fish from these waters. Cod was the most abundant and the most popular. Cod was so important that the people in New England named their area's biggest point of land for the fish, Cape Cod, Massachusetts.

Unfortunately, the world's fishing industry has taken far too many fish from the Grand Banks. There are now too few fish in the waters to support a healthy ecosystem. Governments have passed laws to stop fishing on the Grand Banks. Scientists and fishermen are working hard to find ways to protect the dwindling number of fish that are left there.

B THE TUNA BLUES

Bluefin tuna are one of the largest kinds of fish in the Atlantic Ocean. An adult bluefin can weigh several thousand pounds (more than a small car!). These huge tuna swim across the Atlantic in schools, or groups, of hundreds. They are fast swimmers that like to hunt down squid and fish. Bluefin tuna are also one of the most expensive kinds of fish sold in fish markets. They are so valuable that one fish can *cost* more than a small car! Tuna caught in the Atlantic are frozen and flown to markets in Japan. In Tokyo, a pound (454 grams) of bluefin tuna can cost more than $100.

Sadly, this high value has caused fishers to take far too many bluefins from the Atlantic Ocean. Many people are worried that bluefin tuna may become an endangered species. Scientists are very interested in these beautiful, fast animals because they are so valuable and in potential danger.

Bluefin tuna swim the oceans in large groups, or schools. Some of these fish can weigh more than a ton.

ISLE OF MAN, SEA OF SHARKS

Part of the Atlantic Ocean flows between Ireland and England. Here, it is called the Irish Sea. The largest kind of shark found in cool water swims here. In the summer, both scientists and tourists gather at the Isle of Man—a big island in the Irish Sea—to watch and swim with these sharks. Are these swimming shark-watchers in danger? Not from the sharks, even though they can be as long as a schoolbus and their mouths are big enough to swallow a person whole!

These huge, but not dangerous, sharks are called basking sharks. They have teeth so small they are hard to see. A basking shark eats tiny animals that swim or float near the surface. This feeding shark swims with its mouth wide open. The food-filled water flows into the giant mouth. The water flushes out through the sharks big gill-openings. The tiny food creatures are caught on a net formed inside the shark's mouth from tiny struc-tures called "gill rakers." Later, the shark swallows the tiny animals into its stomach.

The Irish Sea washes up on the rugged shores of southern Ireland.
Inset: **Basking sharks can grow longer than a schoolbus and weigh several tons. Despite their size, they are gentle plankton eaters.**

←The *Titanic* has remained on the Atlantic's cold, dark ocean floor for nearly 90 years.

IS THERE LIFE ON THE TITANIC?

The northern part of the Atlantic Ocean near Canada and England holds danger for ships. Giant icebergs look like floating white mountains drifting down from the north. A ship crashing into an iceberg is like an airplane crashing into a mountain.

One of the most famous shipwrecks of all time occurred in the Atlantic Ocean in 1912. The largest steamship ever built, the *Titanic*, crashed into an iceberg at top speed and sank down to the bottom of the Atlantic. Of the 2,227 people who were aboard, only 705 survived. Some went to the bottom inside the ship.

What was on the bottom of the Atlantic when the *Titanic* hit the mud and came to rest as a dead wreck? Nearly 2.5 miles down (4 kilometers) where the huge ship rests, the water is pitch black and there is no sunlight.

No human had ever laid eyes on the sunken *Titanic* until 1985. Scientists first located the wreckage from the surface. They saw part of the great ship's remains by using a television camera they sent to the bottom. Since then, many trips have been made to the wreck by scientists and filmmakers. They travel in small 2 and 3 person research submersibles that are strong enough to make deep dives. The subs have bright lights, cameras, and robot arms that can be maneuvered to collect animals and samples.

The first dive was made in a research submarine called *Alvin*. Scientists sailed down to the wreckage and viewed the sunken *Titanic* with bright spotlights and video cameras. Long, reddish grasses seem to drape from its hull. Silt particles raining down from the surface covered its decks. The bottom was scattered with dishes, cups, a doll, and other personal belongings amid colonies of sea cucumbers and brittle stars.

What looked like grasses growing on the *Titanic* turned out to be '"whiskers" of rust that formed in the high pressure of the deep sea. Ships that sink in shallow water where sunlight shines are overgrown with seaweeds and sea animals that stick to the hull. But in the darkness of the deep sea no plants grow and the eerie *Titanic* seems bare and lonely.

APPENDIX A:
HOW DO YOU MAP AN OCEAN?

A taxi driver can find an address by using a map and street signs. But how can a sailor find her location on the broad empty ocean? When a boat sails near land, sailors can recognize landmarks. A map, or even a drawing of mountains and cliffs and beaches, can help them find their way. Some of the first maps made by sailors were made on the Red Sea. We know that the Egyptian Queen Hatshepsut sailed the length of the Red Sea 2,500 years ago.

But in the open sea, away from land, there aren't any signs. And how can you make a map of a place that is all ocean?

Here's how—map makers have agreed on two kinds of imaginary lines that cover the Earth. Lines that go from the top of the Earth, at the North Pole, to the bottom of the Earth, at the South Pole, are the lines of "longitude" (LONJ-EH-TOOD). Lines that go around the Earth are the lines of "latitude" (LAT-EH-TOOD). The latitude line that goes around the biggest part of the Earth at its middle is the called the Equator. The half of the Earth above it is the North half of the Earth. The half below the Equator is the South part of the Earth.

The Equator is easy to find on a globe. Map makers also divide the Earth in half with a special longitude line. This line is like an imaginary cut through an orange, slicing it into two halves. Although the "slice" could be made anywhere, map makers have all agreed to put it through the North and South Poles, Greenwich England, and the middle of the Pacific Ocean. This line divides the world into two halves—the West half and the East half. Every line is numbered with degrees because the earth is round like a ball.

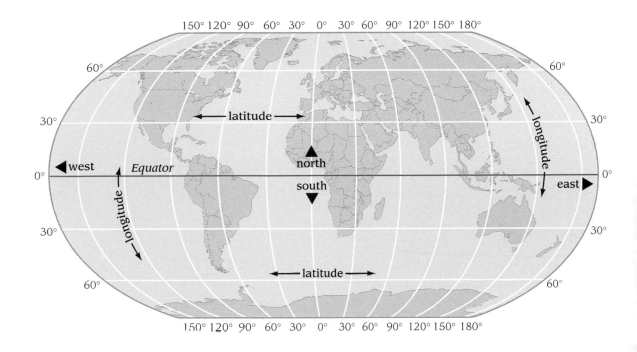

Look at the map of the world above. Locate the longitude line for 60 degrees West. Find the latitude line for 52 degrees North. The two lines will cross at Cape Cod in the Atlantic Ocean.

The place where two lines cross is called a "position." But such lines only appear on maps. Nobody drew them on the ocean like streets. How do sailors find their position? (A sailor who is trying to find a position is called a "navigator.") How does a navigator match up the location of his or her boat with the imaginary lines on his or her map?

By looking at the sky! At any given time, the moon, stars, and the sun are in predictable places. If a navigator knows what time it is and can measure the location of the sun, moon, or a few stars, he or she can find his or her position on Earth.

A new and even easier way has recently been invented. Navigators can use small computers that use satellites instead of stars to find a position of latitude and longitude.

GLOSSARY

barbel A small, soft, fleshy projection on the chin of a fish, such as a cod.

continental shelf The undersea extension of the continent at the edge of an ocean.

current A small or large body of water that is moving slower or faster than the water around it.

Equator The imaginary line of latitude that goes around the waist of the Earth (from east to west).

Gulf Stream A very large warm current that flows from the Caribbean north along the east coast of the United States; parts of it then flow east across the Atlantic to the British Isles.

latitude Imaginary line that goes around the earth from east to west (side to side). Map makers draw them on maps to show where places are located.

longitude Imaginary lines that go around the earth from north to south (up to down). Map makers draw them on maps to show where places are located.

navigation A mathematical way to find exactly where you are (your position) by using latitude and longitude.

poleward The direction toward a pole of the Earth; moving north toward the North Pole; moving south toward the South Pole

population A name scientists give to a large group of a kind of animals that all live together separately from other animals of their same kind.

oceanographer A scientist who studies the ocean and seas, including their currents, waves, plants and animals.

position The exact place where someone or something is, described by latitude and longitude.

sea A great body of seawater that is smaller than an ocean and often almost surrounded by land.

FOR FURTHER INFORMATION

Books

Collins, Jim. *The Bermuda Triangle*. Austin, TX: Raintree/Steck-Vaughn Publishers, 1983.

Halton, Cheryl Mays. *Those Amazing Eels* (Remarkable Animals Series). New York, NY: Dillon Printing Corp., 1990.

Kent, Deborah. *The Titanic* (Cornerstones of Freedom). Danbury, CT: Children's Press, 1993.

Martin, Jim. *Great White Sharks*. Minneapolis, MN: Capstone Press, Inc., 1998.

Mell, Jan. *The Atlantic Grey Whale* (Gone Forever). Morristown, NJ: Crestwood House, 1989.

Papastavrou, Vasilli; Frank Greenway. *Whale* (Eyewitness Books). New York, NY: Knopf, 1993.

Patent, Dorothy Henshaw. *Seals, Sea Lions, and Walruses*. New York, NY: Holiday House, 1990.

Waterlow, Julia. *The Atlantic Ocean* (Seas and Oceans Series). Austin, TX: Raintree/Steck-Vaughn, 1997.

Web Sites

Fantastic Fish Facts—Find amazing answers to common questions about these scaly creatures: www.wh.whoi.edu.faq/fishfaq1a.html

Ocean Color Exploration by NASA—Learn about the factors that determine ocean color with NASA's interactive maps and graphs: www.athena.ivv.nasa.gov/curric/oceans/ocolor/index.html

***Titanic* Exhibit by Britannica**—Explore the history of the great ship at the bottom of the Atlantic: titanic.eb.com/01_01.html

***Titanic* Mock Trial**—Weigh the facts and "testimony" at a mock trial to decide who is to blame for this deadly tragedy: www.andersonkill.com/titanic

Videos

Audubon, *Sharks.* Starring Peter Benchley.
Discovery Channel. *Great White!*
National Geographic. *Secrets of the Titanic.*

INDEX

Photo Credits

Cover: ©Brian Skerry.
Pages 5, 6, 9, 11, 21, 22, 26 and 35: ©Corel; pages 8, 20, and 36: ©PhotoDisc; page 10: ©Corel (top), ©PhotoDisc (bottom); page 13: ©NASA; pages 16-18: ©Andrew J. Martinez; page 23: ©Corel (left), ©IFAW/Innerspace Visions (right); pages 27, 29, and 37: ©Doug Perrine/Innerspace Visions; pages 31–32: ©Andrew J. Martinez, ©Mark Conlin/Innerspace Visions (inset); page 33: ©Andrew J. Martinez (top), ©D. Bay (bottom); page 34: ©Amos Nachoum/Innerspace Visions; page 38: ©Doc White/ Innerspace Visions; page 41: ©Corel, ©Tom Campbell/Innerspace Visions (inset); page 42: ©Ralph White/AP/Worldwide.